THE OLD SOUTH

SMITHMARK

The Image Bank® is a registered trademark of
The Image Bank, Inc.

This edition first published in 1992 by SMITHMARK
Publishers Inc., 112 Madison Avenue,
New York, New York 10016

ISBN 0-8317-0517-5

Printed and bound in Spain

Writers: Bennet & Else Daniels
Designer: Ann-Louise Lipman
Design Concept: Lesley Ehlers
Editor: Joan E. Ratajack
Production: Valerie Zars
Photo Researcher: Edward Douglas
Assistant Photo Researcher: Robert V. Hale
Editorial Assistant: Carol Raguso

Title page: An avenue of stately oaks adorns the approach to Boone Hall Plantation, 8 miles north of Charleston, South Carolina, where visitors have been graciously welcomed since 1681. *Opposite:* At Jamestown Festival Park in Virginia, the ships that brought the English to the New World in 1607 are re-created in loving detail, as seen in this richly carved bollard on the replica of the 100-ton *Susan Constant,* the largest of the three ships on which the settlers sailed.

Our appreciation of the bravery and fortitude of the first European settlers in the South is intensified when viewing the reproductions of the crude homes they built for themselves in Jamestown.

In song and story, in romantic novels and lavish motion pictures, the Old South was a place of beautiful homes, gracious manners, leisured living, fashionable dressing, and polished refinement. A myth? Not completely. Evidence abounds today, more than a century after the end of the Civil War which closed the elegant era, that the Old South of legend was, at least in part, a reality. The plantations, the welcoming town houses, the carefully tended gardens, the elaborate public buildings, the stretches of land kept in their unchanged natural state all affirm to today's visitor that this was a region where once reigned a very special way of life.

"The South is an attitude of mind and a way of behavior just as much as it is a territory," writes historian Francis Butler Simkins. "This section has never lacked a culture as distinctive as its area or its climate. Political, social, and even psychological variations have marked it off from other sections of the country almost as sharply as one European nation is distinguished from another." What is wonderful is how much physical testimony remains today of the formation of that distinctive culture.

The history of the South is tied to its unique geography. It is the only region in the contiguous United States with two coasts.

Top: Upon arriving in the New World, Captain John Smith asserted his leadership abilities and became the driving force in establishing a beachhead; his pioneer spirit is memorialized in this statue at Jamestown. *Right:* The triangular James Fort has been reconstructed in Festival Park, not far from the original Jamestown landing site.

In Williamsburg, Virginia, the flavor of the colonial capital is kept alive by dedicated artisans who practice the crafts of the eighteenth century, such as bookbinding (above) and the production of violins and other stringed instruments (below). *Opposite:* The elegance of the Governor's Palace in Williamsburg, arguably the grandest residence in the colonies at the time it was built, is enhanced by the ten acres of gardens in which it is set.

That fact was key to its early development, for it was explored not in a single drive westward from the pioneers' beachhead but in a variety of directions from a variety of stagings. In 1513, more than a century before the landing of the *Mayflower,* Juan Ponce de León pushed up from Puerto Rico and discovered Florida. Other Spanish explorers followed northward up the peninsula; Hernando de Soto set up an encampment near what is now Tallahassee, and there Christmas was celebrated for the first time on the North American continent in 1539.

In 1562, the French established a short-lived colony in South Carolina, and two years later made a more successful foray into putting down New World roots when 300 Huguenots built the settlement named Fort Caroline in northern Florida. The Spaniards responded by sending a fleet under Don Pedro Menendez de Aviles to set up their own permanent Floridian colony, St. Augustine. It glories in its distinction as the oldest American city. Modern visitors can walk the walls of the Castillo de San Marcos, the fortress begun by the Spaniards in 1672. Still the dominating structure overlooking Matanzas Bay, it has 13-foot-thick walls constructed of a mixture of sand and ground shells.

Top to bottom: Just as George Washington was the first president of the United States, so his Virginia plantation home, Mount Vernon, 16 miles south of Washington, D.C., was one of the first historic houses to be preserved. Maintained since 1858 as a shrine to Washington, it looks much as it did when he died here in 1799.

Just outside Charlottesville, Virginia, Monticello is a personification of Thomas Jefferson, not merely the home of the third president, but his creation: a gem of Enlightenment architecture (Jefferson designed it over four decades) filled with furnishings and inventions that are the fruit of his imaginative mind.

In 1584, after his half-brother Humphrey Gilbert was lost coming back to England from America, Walter Raleigh took up his task of colonizing the New World for Queen Elizabeth. He selected Albemarle Sound's Roanoke Island in what is now North Carolina as the optimum first site. Twice the rigors of the New World defeated the settlers, but the reconstructed fort there now remains evocative for pilgrims, and it will always be remembered as the birthplace of Virginia Dare, the first European child born in North America.

Twenty years later, the English finally succeeded in establishing a permanent settlement in North America. A group of 104 people, operating under a royal charter giving them the right to all the land from New Jersey to the southern tip of Georgia, arrived at what is now Jamestown, Virginia. By 1619, they and the shiploads of adventurers who followed had supplanted military control by establishing the House of Burgesses, the colonies' first representative legislative assembly.

Already the economy was sound; that year 40,000 pounds of tobacco were shipped to London. Glimpses into the very early years of the tobacco economy are available at Flowerdew, one of the earliest plantations, where cultivation began in 1618.

Top: Clover Hill Tavern, established in 1819, is one of the oldest buildings in Virginia's Appomattox Court House, a village that has been restored to look as it did when the Civil War ended in 1865 and what was perceived as the Old South passed into history. *Left:* On street after street of the Old Town section of Alexandria, Virginia, houses from the eighteenth and early nineteenth centuries are now homes for today's families, who shop in the same market square and worship in the same churches that were there in the early days of the nation.

The town hall of Arlington, Virginia, illustrates the enduring aesthetic of the Greek Revival architecture that was so prevalent in the Old South. *Below:* The beautifully maintained clapboard houses of Portsmouth, Virginia, where the Elizabeth River pours into Hampton Roads, are reminders of a local history that reaches back to the construction of the first naval yard here in 1767.

Fredericksburg, Virginia, was home to James Monroe in the 1780's. Many artifacts from his diplomatic and presidential career are on display in his law office, including a wine chest (below, right) used by the president when traveling. Another esteemed local hero was Dr. Hugh Mercer, a brigadier general in the Revolutionary War; his restored apothecary shop (below, left) displays the sorts of herbs and medical instruments he had at his disposal for treating patients.

Wine Chest used by James Monroe while traveling

Virginia prides itself as the home of presidents. One of the most gracious is James Madison's Montpelier, 4 miles from the hamlet of Orange, built by the fourth president's father in 1760. The commanding portico was added in 1793 at the suggestion of Thomas Jefferson. *Below:* In the Tidewater country is Sherwood Forest, John Tyler's home. Built on a spacious James River estate called Walnut Grove when purchased by Tyler in 1842, the central house dates from the colonial period; subsequent additions have brought its full length to 300 feet.

Lafayette Meeks is one of the many soldiers resting for eternity in the Confederate Cemetery at Appomattox.
Left: Peace finally reigns at Manassas, Virginia, the site of the two bloody Civil War battles of Bull Run, a major rail junction deemed so important by both sides that more than 25,000 died in determining its control.

A major component of the southern character is pride in the past: keeping alive the memories of the men and women who forged the history of the area. Statues and monuments in great cities and small—such as these memorials to Robert E. Lee in Charlottesville (above), to Stonewall Jackson in Richmond (below, left), and to the common Confederate soldier in Chancellorsville (below, right)—serve as a constant reminder of the debt the living owe those who came before. *Opposite:* The memories of the past are not just frozen in stone: Large corps of present-day reenacters study the uniforms, weapons, and strategies of the Civil War and re-create major battles for enthusiastic audiences.

A replica of the original windmill built in 1621 with the grist house some ten feet above the field, still grinds grain on windy days. On display are the fruits of extensive archaeological digs on the site, including much evidence of the native American culture that flourished here before the arrival of the Europeans. Nearby at Jamestown Festival Park, a reconstructed Powhatan village brings such artifacts alive, showing the kind of native settlements the English found.

In 1639, Jamestown was prosperous enough to construct a brick church; the tower of that church is still standing today, the only structure left of the original Jamestown. As the town grew stronger, the more venturesome Virginians traveled south. Just across the James River from Jamestown, Arthur Allen built a brick house in 1665. It still welcomes visitors, with its Flemish gables accented by unusual triple chimneys at each end of the principal wing. Others moved on to settle near Raleigh's Roanoke site, and founded Charleston, South Carolina, in 1670.

In 1686, the first seed rice was imported from Madagascar by an imaginative horticulturist, Dr. Henry Woodward, and Carolina growing conditions proved so hospitable that in the

One of the oldest settlements in North Carolina, Edenton is a storehouse of American history. On the green outside the county courthouse (top), colonial towns-women helped push toward a split with England by staging a protest rally against the injustices of the colonial system. By then Cupola House (left), a prize New World example of the Jacobean style, was already 50 years old. Note the characteristic twin exterior chimneys and undersized windows. *Opposite:* The Barker House, moved 40 years ago to its current location on the Edenton waterfront, was built by Thomas Barker, who before the Revolutionary War had served as an agent of the colony in London.

The sunny climate of the South works perfectly with the patience and appreciation of beauty of its residents, resulting in a disproportionate share of the loveliest gardens in America. Not to be missed are the Elizabethan Gardens in Manteo, North Carolina — 10 acres of roses, herbs, and wildflowers carefully selected to ensure that the grounds are abloom all year round. Manteo is the nearest town to Roanoke Island, where the first English settlement in America was established and then mysteriously disappeared.

following decade production burgeoned. The still-standing plantation house, Medway, was begun the same year; from it, 48,000 acres were administered. The wealth produced on these plantations allowed the owners to escape the rural summer heat; with their family fortunes they created the great houses that made a showplace of Charleston— homes built with breezeways and balconies to catch the sea air. That past is still alive in Charleston; in all, more than 2,000 dwellings are now protected by the city's preservationists, most of them still private homes.

Meanwhile the French, who had in 1659 crossed Lake Superior into Wisconsin, began to probe south from there—the spearhead of the third European culture which was to shape the Old South. Jacques Marquette, the Jesuit priest, and Louis Joliet traveled down the Mississippi into Arkansas in 1673; building on their discoveries, René Robert Cavelier, Sieur de La Salle, sailed down the great river to the Gulf of Mexico. French forts followed at such key natural harbors as Biloxi and Mobile. New Orleans was founded in 1718.

The older Southern settlements took on more and more the trappings of established havens of European civilization.

Top to bottom: The Greek Revival style so well exemplified by the Bellamy Mansion in Wilmington, North Carolina, was popular throughout the Old South for both practical and philosophical reasons: The soaring porticos provided shelter from the summer sun, and the broad, welcoming stairways suggested grace and hospitality. The Burgwin-Wright House served as the headquarters for the English general Lord Charles Cornwallis in 1781 and is cherished today for its intricate interior detail. Orton Plantation, 18 miles south of Wilmington, was once a major source of rice for export. Now the fields are a waterfowl refuge, and the grounds are planted with a variety of flowers, crowned of course by the esteemed magnolia.

In colonial days, Tryon Palace in New Bern, North Carolina, was considered the most beautiful home in the colonies, and there are many who would still pay it that tribute. It served as the home of the king's representative in the colony in the 1760's and the first capitol of North Carolina once independence was established. Although Tryon Palace was substantially burned at the end of the eighteenth century, visitors today enjoy a careful reconstruction furnished with authentic antiques and peopled by costumed tour guides.

The oldest building extant in Mecklenburg County, the Hezekiah Alexander house in Charlotte, North Carolina, was built in 1774 and is known locally as "Rock House." Alexander, one of the unsung heroes of the American Revolution, wrote both the first constitution and the first bill of rights for the state of North Carolina. *Below, left:* Near Charlotte, in Pineville, is a grouping of authentic, simple log cabins from the last decade of the eighteenth century. James Polk was born at this site in a similar dwelling; these cabins were moved here as a memorial to the eleventh president. *Right:* Raleigh, North Carolina, is the birthplace of another president, Andrew Johnson. This simple clapboard home was moved in 1975 from its original location in the yard of Casso's Inn to Mordecai Park (opposite page), a historic district with the flavor of Raleigh around the year 1800.

Preceding page: The centerpiece of Mordecai Park is the gracious 1785 home built by Henry Lane and occupied by six generations of his descendants. It is now a vibrant museum reflecting the family's changing tastes as they progressed through the nineteenth century. *This page, above:* Among the 13 monuments that dot the Capitol grounds is one honoring Jackson, Polk, and Andrew Johnson, all elected to the White House as residents of Tennessee, but all born in North Carolina. *Below:* The famous Canova marble statue of George Washington depicted as a Roman warrior was destroyed when the North Carolina Capitol burned in 1831, but a reconstruction now stands proudly in the copper-domed rotunda of the Greek Revival Capitol built two years later.

Just look at the relative comfort of some of the homes associated with George Washington: his own plantation at Mount Vernon which boasted a 900-book library nearby Woodlawn, George and Martha Washington's wedding gift to Lawrence Lewis and Eleanor Parke Custis (his nephew and her daughter from a previous marriage); and Kenmore, the magnificent home of George's sister, Betty, in Fredericksburg, Virginia.

More insight into the elegant plantation life of the colonial period is available at Orton Plantation near Wilmington, North Carolina. Begun in 1735 by the sons of South Carolina governor James Moore, it is set behind two-story-high Doric columns amid cascades of azalea bushes and trees hung with Spanish moss. The impressive Hanover House has today found a home on the grounds of Clemson University in South Carolina, moved there from its original site on the west branch of the Cooper River. Hanover House was constructed in 1716 by Paul de St. Julien on a 1,000-acre tract given to his grand-father by the original holders of the royal charter. Hanover was built between massive chimneys which take up most of each side of the house. It's furnishings show the French Huguenot heritage of its builder, especially in the fine paneling and crewelwork curtains.

Just south of the business district in Winston-Salem, North Carolina, is the restored Moravian village of Old Salem, where the eighteenth-century residents lived a simple God-oriented life and skillfully produced handcrafts. Today a mixture of private homes and museums, the district provides continuous delights to visitors.

Ninety-one original Old Salem buildings survive today. They are unified by stark white walls and unadorned woodwork that raise functionality to the level of art.

Above: The historic district of Charleston, South Carolina, is dominated by its two Episcopal churches: St. Philip's (left), whose steeple (added in 1848, 13 years after the rest of the building was completed) served as a beacon for Confederate ships; and St. Michael's (right), with its original pulpit from the 1750's and pew 43, which seated such notable worshipers as Washington and Lee. *Below:* Charleston lovingly preserves its historic buildings from both the eighteenth and nineteenth centuries, while fitting in a prosperous and appropriate modern commercial life. *Opposite:* The South Carolina Society Hall in Charleston is an artful blending of two key architectural styles: It was created for the group's Huguenot founders in pure Federal style in 1804; its portico is typical of Greek Revival design.

More typically English is Berkeley; on Virginia's James River, it was the family seat of the Harrisons, the family that gave the United States two presidents. Just a few miles to the east, William Byrd II built the much grander Westover, the center of a 179,000-acre agricultural enterprise. That's more than one-quarter the size of Rhode Island!

Arguably the most important family in old Virginia were the Lees. The most significant of their many homes is Stratford Hall, the plantation near Lerty, Virginia. An unusual H-shaped mansion built in the 1730s of brick made on the site and timber cut from the property's forests, it spreads out from a great square central hall that measures 29 feet on each side. Built by Thomas Lee, governor of Virginia as a colony, it was the home of his famous sons: Richard Henry Lee, who goaded the Continental Congress into declaring independence from Britain; Francis Lightfoot Lee, another signer of the Declaration of Independence; Arthur Lee, the emissary of the Continental Congress to France; and William Lee, the fledgling nation's representative to Austria, Prussia, and the Netherlands. Stratford Hall was also the meeting point for the entire extended family. It was here that Robert E. Lee was born of Henry (Light-Horse Harry) Lee and the former Anne Hill Carter.

Top: One of the first theaters in the New World was erected at 135 Church Street in Charleston in 1735, but was replaced nearly a century later by the elegant Planter's Hotel. Still standing, the hotel has been converted back to an eighteenth-century-style theater where local groups put on plays. *Left:* Blocks of public market spaces in the center of Charleston offer a dizzying jumble of shopping, as stalls are claimed by vendors each morning on a first-come basis. Local baked goods, antiques, fine art, kitchenware, and clothing are sold cheek by jowl.

For the southern colonies, perhaps no other event symbolized the transition from frontier outpost to center of civilized pursuits as well as the founding, in 1693, of the College of William and Mary. Two years later, it opened its doors in Williamsburg, and four years after that the town was designated the capital of the colony of Virginia, the seat of the House of Burgesses. Restored and reconstructed, today's Williamsburg embodies the essence of colonial America. The buildings—the grand and the modest, the public and the private—blend together into a pleasing whole because they share a common sense of scale. Guides and craftspeople who stroll the 100-foot-wide Duke of Gloucester Street dressed in eighteenth-century garb on their way to work in the blacksmith, bookbinding, boot, or wig shops add a iiving presence to the illusion.

Whereas Williamsburg and Charleston and St. Augustine remain storehouses of the coastal heritage, other sites capture the style southerners carried with them as they pushed westward. As the colonies became an independent nation, the physical embodiment of their Age of Enlightenment ideals was being created by Thomas Jefferson in Charlottesville, Virginia, at the University of Virginia; at Ash Lawn estate built for James Monroe; and at Jefferson's own

Around every corner, Charleston offers new delights of color, form, and detail. Formed by the confluence of the Ashley and Cooper rivers, the peninsula is filled with old structures still vibrant with life, some serving in their original function as private homes or shops, others imaginatively renovated into more contemporary uses.

The Adam architecture of the home of nineteenth-century merchant Nathaniel Russell (above) and the Caribbean influence seen in the eighteenth-century homes of Rainbow Row (below) testify to the varying influences that resulted in a sophisticated Charleston.

It is the mixing of architectural elements, such as a petite gilded fountain (above) with the formal bulk of the Old Exchange or the Fireproof Building (below, left and right) that gives Charleston its particular human scale.

Preceding page: Kahal Kadosh Beth Elohim's building dates from 1840 and is the oldest synagogue in continuous use in the United States. But the congregation has a longer history: It was founded in 1749 and joined the emerging Reform movement in 1824, the first congregation in America to do so. *This page, above:* Joseph Manigault's house on Meeting Street, dating from 1803, is one of the oldest residences in Charleston. Considered a choice example of the Adam style, it houses priceless early nineteenth-century silver and furniture made by local artisans and is now open to the public. *Below, left:* Gardens were treated as outdoor rooms of antebellum Charleston homes, lavished with as much care—and as integral to the life of the family—as the interior parlors. *Right:* The Fireproof Building, designed by Robert Mills and home of the South Carolina Historical Society, was the first fireproof structure in the country and the pride of Charleston when it was completed in 1827.

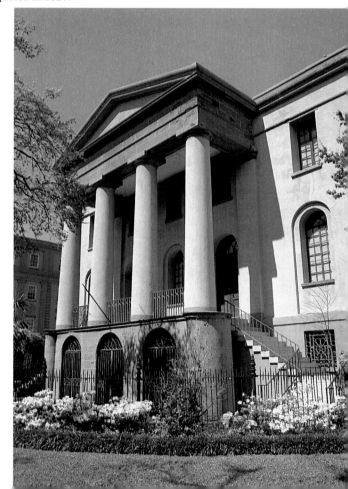

On an island in Charleston harbor accessible only by boat, Fort Sumter is historically significant as the site where the Civil War began on April 12, 1861. Because of its strategic importance, it has been a key defensive fort from the Revolutionary War right up through World War II.

Now at the core of a state park, Rose Hill was a major cotton plantation owned by William H. Gist, governor of South Carolina at the time of its break from the Union. Visitors' programs in its separate kitchen building illustrate nineteenth-century cooking techniques. *Below, left:* Drayton Hall, the oldest surviving home in the Charleston area, is unique among plantation houses open to the public because it is unfurnished, emphasizing the elaborate interior detail work. The atmosphere of antebellum life is particularly acute because the Draytons lived here on and off for seven generations without such modern amenities as electricity, central heating, or indoor plumbing. *Right:* The historic district of Camden, South Carolina, which was established during the Revolutionary War as the interior command post for the entire South, is designed to show the whole range of life in this nationally known center of horsemanship. The buildings run the gamut from simple log cabins to fine, upper-class homes such as the Kershaw-Cornwallis house.

beloved Monticello, a 40-year project not completed until 1809. The legacy continued with Walnut Grove plantation near Spartanburg, begun in 1765, one of the oldest of the mansions in the Carolina up-country; and the grander Meadow Garden in Augusta, Georgia, the 1794 house built by George Walton, a signer of the Declaration of Independence.

At the western edge of Mississippi stands Rosemont, a plantation house built in 1810 with a massive front porch and Palladian windows, and the boyhood home of Jefferson Davis, the president of the Confederacy. Not far away, the city of Natchez, like the older Charleston, cherishes its architectural past. Sixty-four square blocks rising eastward from the Mississippi River contain most of the 500 antebellum homes still standing in the city. Many—including Monmouth, an 1818 Greek revival home with most of its auxiliary buildings still intact, and Dunleith, set in 40 acres of wooded bayous—have arrangements for visitors to stay overnight. One of the most unusual Natchez houses, also taking overnight guests, is Ravennaside, built not for the family to live in but as a party house, where gala entertainments could be given. A musicians' balcony overlooks the polished parquet floor of the ballroom.

In the nineteenth century, Savannah, Georgia, was a bustling port that shipped cotton to Europe and the mills of New England. Factors Walk (top), along the bay, was the center of the trade, where merchants took orders and loaded the cotton. Later the actual buying of the crop was done at the Cotton Exchange, a stately building that is now the home of the nation's oldest Masonic lodge (left), which was organized by Georgia founder James Oglethorpe.

Set off by the blazing azaleas of Johnson Square, Savannah's Greek Revival Christ Episcopal Church, once the home pulpit of John Wesley, is the third structure to serve the congregation at this site. *Below:* Six years after it was completed in 1819, the Owens-Thomas House was the stopping place for the Marquis de Lafayette during his farewell visit to Savannah. Perhaps the greatest accomplishment of architect William Jay, it still awes visitors with its perfectly proportioned portico and interior detail.

Northeast of Calhoun, Georgia, history buffs have reconstructed New Echota, the capital of the Cherokee nation from 1817 until 1839. The Native Americans in New Echota developed an elaborate government structure based on that of the United States, with a legislature and a supreme court (above), in which a panel of three judges heard cases. Moved to the 220-acre historic site as part of the reconstruction is the Vann Tavern (below), originally built on another site by the Cherokee in 1805.

Due south of Natchez in Louisiana is a string of Mississippi River plantation mansions. Clustered together are Bocage, Belle Hélène, Nottoway (with 64 rooms, the largest plantation house of them all), Tezcuco, and a half dozen other survivals of the plantation houses which sported a busy Creole social whirl in the mid-nineteenth century.

Perhaps the gem of the group is Houmas House. Visitors are delighted with original American-crafted furniture; hinges, door-knobs, tiles, and ceiling sconces imported from France and Germany; and a sweeping, curved central staircase that seems made for the rustle of silk and crinoline. The exterior is an elegant, pillared, white square with rounded dormers peeping out of the hip roof, set amid moss-hung live oaks, absolutely prototypical of its neighbor-hood—and of the atmosphere that made the producers of *Hush, Hush, Sweet Charlotte* decide to film the movie there. This was the center of sugar growing in America, and of a distinctive way of life. The houses were the center of a self-contained hamlet; they were flanked by, among other build-ings, offices, guest houses, and, typically, a *garçonnière* for the young bachelors who congregated there and who were so essential to the gallant balls and parties.

Top: The most famous leaders of the Confederacy—Robert E. Lee, Stonewall Jackson, and Jefferson Davis—are memo-rialized in relief on Stone Mountain, 16 miles east of Atlanta. *Right:* The South honors not only leaders but all those who rallied to the Confederate cause. Soldiers who fought in the battles of Pigeon Hill and Cheatham Hill are remembered in the now quiet National Battlefield Park at Kennesaw Mountain, Georgia.

At Houmas House the *garçonnière* is octagonal, with the ground floor nothing but a series of arches and the bedrooms on the second floor.

The journey to find the Old South would then dip down from the Baton Rouge area to New Orleans at the mouth of the Mississippi, a town where the exuberance of life has long been given a high priority. Today many of the same buildings that made the city so impressive in the early 1800s are still there: the 1795 Cabildo, from which the Spaniards ruled Louisiana and the French turned over the territory to the United States; the nearby Presbytère, first begun in 1793 and for many years a courthouse; St. Louis Cathedral; and the Ursuline Convent, originally dedicated in 1734 and now the home of the archdiocesan archives.

All those buildings are in the Vieux Carré, a quarter that is a kind of huge museum, an alive, thriving gallery. The evidence of the Old South on display there includes not only the jewels of the Spanish era but such other monuments as the Beauregard-Keyes House of 1826, the Hermann-Grima House, where Creole cooking demonstrations are given every Thursday on the open hearth in the outlying kitchen building, and the Italianate house at 1118 Royal Street, built in 1832.

The early history of the South was forged not just by English settlers but also by the Spanish and the French. Perhaps the strongest Spanish influence can be seen in St. Augustine, Florida, the oldest permanent settlement in the United States. The old Spanish Quarter has been reconstructed in an approach mindful of colonial Williamsburg. Dominating the quarter and the harbor itself is an authentic structure from the days of Spanish dominance, the Castillo de San Marcos. Begun in 1672, the citadel's 12-foot-thick walls have withstood assaults by both humans and nature. It was used as a military post well into the twentieth century.

The pink-stuccoed Government House is just one of the mementoes of the Spanish past in St. Augustine, where the attractions include the oldest house in the United States, the oldest store, and the oldest wooden schoolhouse. *Below:* Near Pensacola, Florida, the Gulf barrier of Santa Rosa is a spindly sandbar boasting both unspoiled beaches and historic sites, the most significant of which is Fort Pickens. Built in 1834, it was held by Union troops, despite repeated Confederate assaults, throughout the Civil War. The arches of this masonry construction are considered typical of nineteenth-century military architecture.

Montgomery, Alabama, was the first capital of the Confederacy and the place where "Dixie" was written and adopted as the official battle anthem of the Southern cause. This heritage is kept alive in many fine residences now operated as museums, including the Rice-Semple-Haardt House, the only antebellum home in the capital still on its original site. *Below:* Tuskegee Institute in Tuskegee, Alabama, has the distinction of having its entire campus designated a National Historical Site. Included on the site established by Congress in 1974 is the impressive Grey Columns mansion. *Opposite:* The Alabama Capitol, set among flowers and statuary, dates from 1851, and was a replacement for the legislative building that burned down two years earlier. It was the site of Jefferson Davis's inauguration as president of the Confederacy.

But for a visitor, the recurring image of the Old South will come not just from the built environment, but from the unbuilt—the nature preserves which prove what a luxuriant, fertile land this is. Thanks to that soil and climate, notes psychologist Robert Coles, "The growth is different; tropical plants and palm trees, the famous wisteria and symbolic magnolia. The water is particularly abundant and rich in its variety: wide rivers, their tributaries weaving through the entire region, and the still smaller bayous, and canals, and the swamps with the mist over them. Lakes are everywhere, and much of the oceanside shows a tropical green bank when it touches the shore."

For example, the Delta National Forest near Yazoo City, Mississippi, is a 60,000-acre haven for deer, wild turkey, and woodcock. At Horseshoe Bend National Park in Alabama, where the Tallapoosa River twists around in an awesome U shape, the tree-covered hills, ablaze with wildflowers nine months a year, define the very essence of the Piedmont. Some 20 miles wide and 40 miles long,

Mobile, Alabama, continues to exude a special charm, drawing on its Gulf-front location and its French and Spanish heritage: It was founded in 1711 by the Sieur de Bienville, became a Spanish possession in 1780, and did not become a legal part of the United States until 1813. The Richards-DAR House, renowned for its elaborate, gleaming white ironwork with medallions representing each of the four seasons, is one of the most prized sites in the city.

Oakleigh, the jewel of Mobile's Garden District, stands on the highest ground in the original settlement. A five-year project begun in 1833 for cotton broker James W. Roper, it has a first floor built of bricks made right on the Savannah Street property. *Below:* The Bragg-Mitchell House on Mobile's Springhill Avenue remains one of the city's most elegant. It was built in 1855 by Judge John Bragg, brother of the famous Confederate general Braxton Bragg.

Above, left: Tuskegee Institute was founded by Booker T. Washington in 1881 as a trade school for African Americans and is a monument to his determination and pioneering spirit. On the campus, the life-size statue of Washington shows him lifting the "veil of ignorance" that limited opportunities for former slaves. *Right:* When the French ruled Mobile, their power was centered in Fort Condé, now reconstructed as a center for visitors, with guides dressed as early eighteenth-century soldiers. *Below:* In contrast, Mobile's star-shaped Fort Morgan is authentic, dating from the early nineteenth century, the best preserved of the string of military bulwarks that encircled Mobile Bay.

Fort Massachusetts, on West Ship Island in the Gulf of Mexico south of Biloxi, Mississippi, is a mecca for tourists who want to capture the flavor of military life in the mid-nineteenth century. A pet project of Jefferson Davis when he was the U.S. secretary of war, it was officially authorized by Congress in 1857.

Above, left: The unusual ball-and-peg ornamentation on the Brielmaier House in Biloxi offers a haven from the southern sun and has made the structure the obvious choice for the city's visitors' center. *Right:* Long before he entered politics and was elected mayor of Jackson, Mississippi, in 1862, Charles Henry Manship gained a reputation as one of the city's greatest building craftsmen—a talent that reached its fullest expression when he built his own Gothic-style home. *Below:* Since 1841, Mississippi governors have lived in this mansion, which also served as headquarters for Sherman during the Union occupation of Jackson. Today the building serves a dual purpose: The governor's family lives in a new back wing, and the original building, filled with superb nineteenth-century furnishings, is open to the public as a museum. *Opposite:* Following a recent renovation, the Mississippi Capitol, which was strongly influenced by the federal Capitol in Washington, glows like new.

Some of the South's finest mansions can be found in Natchez, Mississippi. Dunleith (above), set in a 40-acre park and furnished with fine antiques from France and England, and Edgewood (below) are among the most elegant homes in the upper city. *Opposite:* Built in 1818, Natchez's Monmouth served as the home of Mexican War hero John Anthony Quitman. It is now a Civil War museum, and like Dunleith, does an active business as an inn, with spacious suites furnished with authentic antiques.

Georgia's Okefenokee Swamp presents unspoiled freshwater wetlands, moss-covered cypresses reflected in brown waters, with yellow spaddock and white bay tree flowers adding sudden, unexpected flashes of color to the dark, fairy-tale surroundings.

As impressive as the unchanged preserves are the gardens where the region's botanical riches are carefully nurtured. It is an old heritage: Look at the Trustees' Garden in Savannah, on the site of the original experimental garden begun by James Oglethorpe. In 1733, he planted seeds he had brought from London's Chelsea Physic Garden in hopes of creating vineyards and crops of medicinals in the New World. There is even an herb house in the garden which is probably the oldest building in Georgia still standing. The peach trees in Trustees' Garden are said to be the original ones in the colony.

The botanical gardens in Birmingham have been described as "67 acres of horticultural heaven"; among the displays is a formal Japanese garden. Just west of Jackson, Mississippi, is Mynelle Gardens, with 1,000 varieties of plants but perhaps most interesting for its tropical area, which hints at what the South may have looked like before the Europeans arrived. In Sumter, South Carolina, the Swan Lake Iris Gardens contrast the pastels of the irises and camellias with the onyx-black waters of the lake.

Top: The construction of Longwood, the largest octagonal house in the United States, was interrupted by the Civil War and the interior work on the upper levels was never completed. Despite that fact, Longwood has become a Natchez showplace as its original owner—Haller Nutt, a cotton planter who was quick to embrace modern agricultural methods—intended it to be.

Preceding page, bottom: Much of the distinctiveness of the South comes from its natural attributes: the rich soil and the lush vegetation of the subtropics. The wilderness road known as the Natchez Trace looks much as it did when Ohio traders used it to walk back north after having sailed merchandise-laden flatboats down the Mississippi to Natchez or New Orleans, where they sold the entire lot, goods and barge. *This page:* The strategic location of Vicksburg, Mississippi, on a bluff overlooking a bend in the Mississippi River, made it a key objective of both Civil War armies and the site of a fierce 47-day siege. Today a national military park allows visitors to retrace the campaign and includes a cemetery, mute testimony to the toll the battle extracted.

The raised cottage in the Longfellow-Evangeline State Commemorative Area, in St. Martinville, Louisiana, is typical of Creole dwellings on plantations in the bayou country. *Right:* At Henderson, west of Baton Rouge in the heart of Louisiana's Cajun country, travelers can board pontoon boats for a tour of the Atchafalaya Basin, where the flora, fauna, and enveloping stillness transport them back in time to the swampland that faced the earliest settlers.

Travelers seek out not just the glories of the Old South but also the shrines of its destruction, for all the states of the Confederacy are peppered with battlefield monuments to that terrible conflict. Every square mile was fought over, and on many, fierce battles were won one year only to be lost the next. On an island in Charleston Harbor, the preserved Fort Sumter is where the conflagration began. The two-day battle at Chickamauga, Georgia, was perhaps the fiercest of the war, and the park preserving that battlefield is both the oldest and the largest military park in the United States. At Petersburg, Virginia, the battlefield park commemorates the final major battle of the war. A battlefield monument at Vicksburg National Military Park in Mississippi carries a frieze of a Confederate and a Union soldier shaking hands in brotherhood.

There's no question that the South has risen again. Today modern skyscrapers dominate Richmond and Atlanta and New Orleans, sun-seeking Americans flock to make new lives along the Gulf Coast crescent, and international commerce and industry prosper. But the scent of honeysuckle and magnolia still hangs in the night air, while manners and manors combine to produce a graceful life in the New South that is reminiscent of the Old.

Top to bottom: Along the Mississippi between Baton Rouge and New Orleans is one of the premier stretches of preserved plantation houses from the Old South. Oak Alley is one of the most renowned, as it was used as the setting for the television movie *The Long Hot Summer*; the two dozen trees that give the house its name are nearly 300 years old. The fanciful San Francisco is elaborately decorated to emulate the steamboats that carried passengers up and down the great river. Houmas House, the westernmost of the trio, gained fame as the location for the movie *Hush . . . Hush Sweet Charlotte.*

All the ingredients that blended to create the Old South—English, French, and Spanish influences; the grace of plantation life; and the bustle of commerce—converge in exciting New Orleans. Around every corner in the Vieux Carré is a new delight: Napoleon House (above, left), which quite possibly serves the best muffuletta (a sort of Creole hoagie) in town; the long-famous Old Absinthe House (above, right), where money and business cards paper the walls; and the enticing Court of the Two Sisters (below).

The peace treaty ending the War of 1812 was actually signed before the Battle of New Orleans, in which Andrew Jackson won acclaim for his brilliance leading the U.S. troops in the confrontation. In recognition, his statue was placed in the park in front of St. Louis Cathedral, and the land, known as Place d'Armes, was renamed Jackson Square. *Below:* In the cemetery adjoining the cathedral are the above-ground graves typical of New Orleans, a city so low lying that water wells up with any deep digging.

Every year before the start of Lent, New Orleans lets loose in a carnival that sweeps together all the diversity of the city's residents and its visitors, resulting in a days-long, world-famous party. Mardi Gras is colorful and exuberant, mixing the spirit of the Old South with that of the new.

Index of Photography

All photographs courtesy of The Image Bank except where indicated *.